THE LIBRARY OF
AMERICAN
LIVES AND TIMES™

MARQUIS DE LAFAYETTE

French Hero
of the American Revolution

Gregory Payan

J.Albert Adams
Academy Media Center

The Rosen Publishing Group's
PowerPlus Books™
New York

To my mom, for her much-valued opinion,
and to Casey Elizabeth, for her patience

Published in 2002 by The Rosen Publishing Group, Inc.
29 East 21st Street, New York, NY 10010

First Edition

Library of Congress Cataloging-in-Publication Data

Payan, Gregory.
Marquis de Lafayette : French hero of the American Revolution /
by Gregory Payan.— 1st ed.
    p. cm. — (The library of American lives and times)
Includes bibliographical references and index.
ISBN 0-8239-5733-0
1. Lafayette, Marie Joseph Paul Yves Roch Gilbert Du Motier, marquis
de, 1757–1834—Juvenile literature. 2. Generals—United
States—Biography—Juvenile literature.
3. United States. Army—Biography—Juvenile literature.
4. Statesmen—France—Biography—Juvenile literature.
5. United States—History—Revolution, 1775–1783—Participation,
French—Juvenile literature. 6. Generals—France—Biography—Juvenile
literature. 7. France. Armâee—Biography—Juvenile literature.
 [1. Lafayette, Marie Joseph Paul Yves Roch Gilbert Du Motier, marquis
de, 1757–1834. 2. Generals. 3. Statesmen. 4. United
States—History—Revolution, 1775–1783—Participation, French.]
 I. Title. II. Series.
E207.L2 P26 2002
944.04'092—dc21

00-013062

Manufactured in the United States of America

CONTENTS

1. Who Was Marquis de Lafayette?

French by birth, but with an American heart, Marquis de Lafayette was one of the most important people involved in the American Revolution. Lafayette was commissioned as a major general in the Revolutionary War. He was only nineteen, but on the battlefield he displayed leadership and maturity beyond his years. He was not content with only military glory, however. Marquis de Lafayette was also an important political figure in France for fifty years after returning from America after the war. Throughout his life, he successfully used his words and actions to change things that he felt were wrong.

While fighting in the American Revolution, Lafayette convinced France to aid the Americans in their battle against the British. The Americans could not have won the war without the much-needed money, troops, and supplies that the French provided. Lafayette was also valuable to the Americans for what

Opposite: This eighteenth-century portrait by an unknown artist portrays Marquis de Lafayette in his military uniform. On his hat there is a red, white, and blue piece of cloth, as well as plumes of the same three colors. These colors not only symbolize the new nation Lafayette helped to create in America, but also they symbolize his hope that the French Revolution would unite the government and the people of France in the cause of liberty.

he represented. Lafayette was a Frenchman with no ties to America. All he had was a strong belief in what Americans were fighting for. The Americans fought the British despite being outnumbered and having few supplies. If they were going to win against the more powerful British, they would have to win on heart and inspiration. Lafayette's presence in the war provided those. The American people and the Continental army knew that halfway across the world there were people and nations that supported them and believed in their cause.

Lafayette had a saying he liked to use, "Why not?" or, *"Cur non?"* in French. From the time he was a young boy to the time of his death, he believed anything was possible. He lived his whole life believing that he could influence people and government for the good of society. Throughout his life, he sacrificed important positions in French government to help those he felt were oppressed. During the course of his life, he would participate in three revolutions—one in America and two in France.

France was in political turmoil for most of Lafayette's adult life. There was constant change in government and violent protests were common. Lafayette often put himself in danger by speaking in the middle of riots, armed only with his voice. He would speak against any leader whose actions did not live up to his words and was unafraid of spurring protests

This is Lafayette's crest. It has a red-and-gold shield upon a field of blue and silver castles. There is a knight's headplate at the top, crested with a crown with a horse, reined, with flower decorations at the side. Lafayette's motto, *Cur Non?*, is at the bottom.

among the people, yet he could also be a calming influence when it was needed.

As with many people who have had strong opinions throughout history, he was loved at times and hated at other times. Lafayette was almost always opposed to those who ruled France and he was constantly trying to change French government to make it better for the people. He believed a government was useless unless the people had a voice in how they were governed. His entire life was dedicated to this cause.

2. Lafayette's Early Life

Marie Joseph Paul Yves Roch Gilbert du Motier de Lafayette was born on September 6, 1757, in the French province of Auvergne. Throughout his early years, he was just Gilbert to his family and friends. Later on, he would become the Marquis or just Lafayette. Gilbert was born into a family who were considered members of the nobility in their province. On the day of his birth, a group of important townspeople had gathered at the home for his baptism. Gilbert's father, Colonel Michel de Lafayette, was fighting for France in the Seven Years' War against England when Gilbert was born. Sadly, Gilbert would never meet his father. Colonel Michel de Lafayette died at the age of twenty-seven in the Battle of Minden on August 1, 1759, two years after Gilbert's birth. His death, while noble, would be in vain. In 1763, France would lose the war to England and her allies.

After his father died, Gilbert's mother moved to her parents' home in Paris. Gilbert, however, stayed at their country home with his paternal grandmother and two

This is a portrait of Marquis de Lafayette as a young man. Marquis is a French term of nobility. It refers to a nobleman ranking just below a duke and above an earl or a count. Lafayette spent much of his youth training to be a member of the upper class.

aunts. Gilbert's mother had never wanted to live in the country and always preferred city life. She had only lived in Auvergne because of her marriage to Gilbert's father.

After his father's death in the war, Gilbert's family applied for cash assistance from King Louis XV so they could properly raise and educate Gilbert. During this time period in France, the families of officers killed in battle would often get money from the government. Because women did not work, men were relied on for income. King Louis XV reviewed their request and agreed that the family should get some money to help bring up Gilbert. He granted them a stipend of six hundred livres, about three thousand dollars, per year to help educate Gilbert until he became an adult.

Gilbert was a very intelligent child. The same priest who baptized him taught him to read, write, and pray. He also introduced Gilbert to Latin. Gilbert was educated not only in typical things like math and history, but also in the importance of values such as courage and dignity.

While growing up with his grandmother and his aunts, Gilbert heard many great stories of military life, including stories about his father. It was during his childhood that Gilbert began to develop a love of the military and the glory it could bring. As a child, he dreamed of defending the town peasants from imaginary beasts. A werewolf was rumored to be terrorizing

This oil painting of Lafayette's father, Michel Christophe du Motier, Marquis de Lafayette, was done by an anonymous French artist in 1754, just four years before he died in the Battle of Minden. Gilbert was only two when his father died, so his only memories of him were based on the stories told to him by his aunts and grandmother.

*In France during
the 1760s, a farm laborer
made about fifty livres a year,
a servant twenty. Although the amount
given to Lafayette's family by the king
was not an incredible amount of money, six
hundred livres a year was very generous.
To educate Gilbert, Lafayette's family
would receive in one month what
a farm laborer would
earn in a year.*

people in his town and he often looked through the woods around the castle hoping to come across it. It can be said that this was the beginning of Gilbert's desire to help defend the weak against those more powerful. Gilbert was very smart and wanted to be great in whatever he did. When he got older, he didn't just want to be successful; he also wanted to be considered a war hero.

At age eleven, Gilbert moved back in with his mother in Paris. Here he would start training to be an officer and also take classes to prepare him for his future wealth. Although his father's family was not very

This engraving shows a general view of Paris. It is by Johann Georg Ringlin, a mapmaker and engraver from Augsburg, who lived from 1691 to 1761. Paris is shown as a bustling metropolis, and the ship in the foreground indicates that it was prosperous in trade, as well. The tall spires in the skyline are probably churches, symbolizing that the people of Paris were pious and just.

wealthy, his mother's family was. When Gilbert was considered an adult, he would share in this wealth. At this time, people who had a lot of money were known as aristocrats. They attended dinners, dances, and assorted functions with other members of the upper class. Once Gilbert was a little older, he would be expected to behave in a certain way at such events. If he did not, he would embarrass himself and his family.

After Gilbert moved to Paris, his mother enrolled him in one of the best schools in the city, the College du Plesis. Classes were taught in both Latin and French. He was excellent at Latin but history was his favorite subject.

In 1770, when he was thirteen, Gilbert's mother died after an illness. Illnesses that are easily treated today with medication or a trip to the doctor were very dangerous in the eighteenth century. It was more than two hundred years ago and medicine was not very advanced. Within one week, his mother's father died, as well. Most accounts say that he died of a broken heart.

Gilbert's inheritance after the death of his grandfather made him a very rich boy. Gilbert would receive an annual stipend of 120,000 livres ($600,000) from his grandfather's estate. In the course of one week, everything had changed for Gilbert. He went from playing in his grandfather's home to owning it.

During his teenage years, Gilbert attended the most prestigious military school in France, the Academie de Versailles. At the Academie he learned, with the king's grandson, to ride horses and perform military drills. He maintained a good stable and was a fine horseman.

Now that Gilbert was a wealthy young aristocrat, his great-grandfather and legal guardian, the Comte de la Riviere, began to arrange Gilbert's wedding. At that time, the children of aristocratic families always had their marriages arranged. By doing this, the rich could make sure there was little interaction between classes. They could guarantee that a wealthy family member would marry a wealthy member of another family. His great-grandfather wanted him to marry someone with high standing in society. Therefore the Comte de la Riviere chose a daughter of

Madame de La Fayette

From a Miniature in the possession of the Family

This 1894 hand-colored etching of Adrienne Lafayette was done by Albert Rosenthal from a miniature that the Lafayette family had in their possession. Adrienne married Lafayette when she was fourteen. During their marriage, she and Lafayette worked to free people who were enslaved. The couple bought two slave plantations in South America with the purpose of freeing the people and distributing the land to them. Adrienne worked very hard to educate them in reading and writing, as well as in the proper operation of plantations.

the Ayer-Noailles family, one of the wealthiest families in France. He felt that their twelve-year-old daughter, Adrienne, would make a perfect wife for Gilbert.

Gilbert was fifteen and on vacation in Chauviniac when he learned of his great-grandfather's selection. Gilbert had no choice in the matter but he was very pleased when he saw Adrienne. She was a very pretty girl. When Adrienne's mother was informed of the marriage plans, she insisted they wait at least two years to marry because they were too young. By that time, Adrienne would be able to determine for herself if she wanted to marry Gilbert. During those two years, Adrienne did, in fact, fall in love with Gilbert. They would often meet for walks, carriage rides, and occasionally to spend time together in the family mansion.

Adrienne and Gilbert were wed on April 11, 1774. Gilbert was sixteen and Adrienne was fourteen. Though they were young, this was an acceptable age to get married in the eighteenth century. Gilbert was tall and had red hair. He was very thin, awkward, and unsophisticated. Adrienne was also tall, but she was beautiful and graceful. She had blue eyes and blonde hair. Although they were two very different people, Adrienne seemed to love Gilbert very much. Before he was married, Gilbert had wealth but not much power. Now he had both. There were many wealthy families in France, but the Ayer-Noailles family was among the wealthiest and they had a lot of influence.

3. Lafayette Learns of the American Cause

Soon after Gilbert and Adrienne married, Louis XV died and Louis XVI succeeded him. Gilbert would receive a military commission in the Noailles Dragoons, a regiment in the French army, through Louis XVI. Adrienne's father had tried to get Gilbert a commission earlier but Louis XV had refused. At this time, the ruler of France sold military commissions. Even though Adrienne's father had plenty of money, Louis XV felt Gilbert was too young. Louis XVI was more open to persuasion and wanted the money that he would collect for granting Gilbert a captain's rank. He did not care how old Gilbert was. Late in 1774, a young Gilbert joined the Dragoons regiment in the Lorraine region of eastern France. He was granted all the privileges of a captain's rank but could not take command of his company for two years because of his young age. Gilbert had just turned seventeen.

While completing their military obligations, the young men of the French military socialized a lot. They played tennis, badminton, football, and other sports.

King Louis XVI, who granted Lafayette his rank as captain, lived from 1754 to 1793 and was king from 1774 to 1792. He was married to Marie Antoinette in 1770. In the early years of his reign, he appointed competent ministers to rule France. Unfortunately he lacked leadership abilities and was easily swayed by his wife and the wealthy courtiers who opposed many reforms proposed by his ministers.

They also often gambled. Gilbert participated in sports but was not very good at them. He was still quite shy and he hated gambling, something that all of his friends seemed to love. Despite his lack of interest in or talent for the activities that most young men his age participated in, Gilbert was well liked by everyone who associated with him.

French officers were almost always from aristocratic families. Society expected young men from wealthy families to join the military and fight for France. Most young officers looked forward to war. They had wealth, but if they were successful in a war, they would be heroes for the rest of their lives. Young Frenchmen grew up expecting to be war heroes. Most of their time was spent waiting for this opportunity to prove themselves. Without war, many young men, like Lafayette, got bored.

In 1775, across the Atlantic Ocean, a group of British colonies were causing a bit of a stir. The American colonies established by the British were not happy with the rules and taxes that were being forced on them. A series of events over the last ten years had forced the colonists to take action. In 1765, the British had passed the Stamp Act. The British were trying to raise money by taxing the colonists on papers, cards, almanacs, and dice. The Boston Tea Party, in 1773, further increased tension. The colonists dumped more than 340 chests of tea belonging to the British East India

Company into Boston Harbor. They were again protesting what they felt was unfair taxation. In response, the British passed the Intolerable Acts, which were four punishments for colonial defiance of laws that had been passed earlier. This brought about the formation of the Continental Congress in late 1774. Here the colonies united in their protests against Britain. They decided they needed to work together to throw off British rule.

In April 1775, British general Thomas Gage sent a force from Boston to destroy American rebel military stores in Concord, Massachusetts, and the war had

This hand-colored illustration shows the British retreating from Concord and Lexington back toward Boston. The road that the army retreated on is known as Battle Road because of the bloody skirmishes fought between the British and the colonists during the retreat.

begun. The colonies had decided they no longer wanted Britain ruling over them if they had no voice in how they would be governed. They were beginning their war for independence, a war that would later be known as the American Revolution.

In August 1775, several months after fighting broke out in America, Gilbert and his brother-in-law attended a gathering that made a great impression on them. It was a dinner given by the Duke de Broglie, marshal of France. Here, Gilbert first learned of the American colonies' demand for full representation in Parliament. He also learned that the colonists had unanimously elected George Washington as their general and commander in chief. Washington would lead an army against the British so the colonies could gain their independence. After the dinner, Gilbert would say, "As soon as I knew of this quarrel, my heart was committed to it and I thought only of joining my colors to it."

Gilbert closely followed the American situation for the rest of 1775. Unfortunately, as an officer in the French military, he was not permitted to fight in another country's war unless France was directly involved. As 1775 came to a close, Gilbert was about to receive good news. In December 1775, Adrienne gave birth to a baby girl named Henriette.

In 1776, Louis XVI appointed the Comte de Saint-Germain as minister of war for France. It would soon become apparent that his appointment would be a huge

M. LE COMTE DE SAINT GERMAIN.
Lieutenant Général des Armées du Roi
Com.ᵈᵉ de l'Ordre R.ᵃˡ et Milit.ᵉ de S.ᵗ Louis

Comte de Saint-Germain, born around 1710, was quite accomplished in music, history, and chemistry. He was made the French minister of war in 1776 by Louis XVI. Saint-Germain became unpopular with generals because he tried to reorganize the army after Frederick the Great's Prussian army, known for being extremely strict in its discipline and drilling of soldiers.

problem for Gilbert. The Comte de Saint-Germain began to totally reform the military. One of his first targets was the removal of medium-ranking officers from the ranks. Most of them had been promoted through monetary and political influence without having actually served in a war. Gilbert fell into this category. He, along with many others, was removed from active service and placed on reserve at half pay on June 11, 1776. Unless war broke out, his dream of military glory seemed unlikely. Now, more than ever, he yearned to go to America to fight.

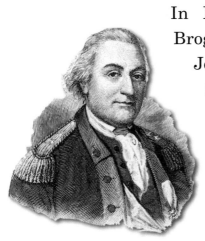

Baron Johann DeKalb was killed in the Battle of Camden during the American Revolution. His tombstone reads: "Here lies the remains of Baron DeKalb—A German by birth, but in principle, a citizen of the world."

In December 1776, the Duke de Broglie introduced his protégé, Baron Johann DeKalb, and Gilbert to Silas Deane, the American delegate to France. Deane was trying to get French political support and supplies for the American cause. To do this, he promised high rank and money to French officers willing to fight in America. Even though the French government did not approve, the sympathetic de Broglie sent Deane his most trusted officers, including the Baron DeKalb, who was given a rank of major general and a stipend of twelve thousand livres. DeKalb was a German mercenary who fought in the French army during the Seven Years' War. He was well respected and was a good field general.

Silas Deane desperately wanted Gilbert to go with DeKalb. Despite Gilbert's youth and inexperience, Deane promised him the rank of major general, the same rank that he had given DeKalb. Deane hoped King Louis XVI would participate in the war on America's behalf. He thought that by bringing one of the most wealthy and powerful people in France to America, he could influence the French government to get involved. France was already providing some aid to America in the interest of trade. They were reluctant to do more because open support of America meant the risk of war with England in Europe. After all, not too long ago they had been defeated by England in the Seven Years' War.

Gilbert was nineteen and viewed a trip to America as an adventure that could bring him the military glory he desired so much. Once he decided to make the journey, Gilbert had to figure out how he would get there. He knew the king and his father-in-law would not want him to go. Formal permission was requested from the king and was denied. In spite of this, Gilbert was determined to travel to America anyway.

In early 1777, Gilbert secretly purchased a cargo ship, *La Victoire*. He and DeKalb would use it to sail to

LOS PEYNOS de ESPANA Y PORTUGAL.

American shores as soon as they could. Soon after Gilbert purchased the ship, his father-in-law and the king learned of the plan. The king said anybody who assisted them in their journey would be put in jail. Gilbert knew it would be impossible to leave from France as they had originally planned. People were now afraid to assist them. Determined to leave anyway, Gilbert had the ship moved to Las Pasajes, in northern Spain. After encountering more problems, he secretly went to Spain to board the ship. On April 20, 1777, he finally set sail for America with DeKalb and a small crew. Gilbert was not able to say good-bye even to Adrienne, though she was pregnant with his second child.

Opposite: This is a 1777 map of Spain. Lafayette was forced to move his ship to Las Pasajes, Spain, highlighted in blue, when his father-in-law and the king got in the way of his original plans to go to America. It was illegal for a French soldier to fight in a war in which France was not directly involved. In essence, Lafayette was forced to smuggle himself and a few other men out of the country.

4. Setting Sail for America

Gilbert was no longer a boy. He was going across the ocean to serve as a major general in a war. He was now Lafayette, the French marquis who was to help lead the Americans to victory.

The journey across the Atlantic Ocean was a tough one. Although ships were sturdy at this time, they moved very slowly, using only wind currents for power. Crossing the ocean was also boring and could take any-where from six weeks to three months. This journey would take more than seven weeks, but to Lafayette it seemed like seven years. He was terribly seasick the whole time. The sea shook *La Victoire* so violently that men had to be tied to their hammocks when they attempted to sleep. Lafayette spent most of the time with DeKalb, working on his English. In one letter to Adrienne he stated, "I won't give you a diary of my voyage. Here

Opposite: This is an image of Lafayette's departure by Gustave Olaux. It shows Lafayette's ship, *La Victoire*. Traveling by sea was never easy in the eighteenth century, but Lafayette and his crew suffered an especially rough passage.

the days follow each other, and, what is worse, seem like each other. Always the sky, always the water, and the same the following day."

Despite setting sail for Philadelphia, the ship's captain, unsure of where he was going, arrived about eight hundred miles (1,288 km) south of Lafayette's target port. British ships were sailing up and down the American coast, and the captain refused to go north without someone familiar with the surrounding area. On June 13, 1777, Lafayette's group finally arrived on the American shore in Georgetown, South Carolina. Lafayette, DeKalb, and their small group traveled

This is a 1767 map of South Carolina. In 1777, Lafayette and his men landed in Georgetown, highlighted in blue, then spent several weeks in and around Charleston, highlighted in orange. Soon they had to march hundreds of miles (km) north to reach Philadelphia, their destination.

through swamps for several hours and finally arrived at the plantation home of Major Benjamin Huger. Instead of finding welcoming arms, they were greeted with musket fire when they first arrived on his property. Lafayette quickly explained to Major Huger who they were and the homeowner apologized for firing on them. Major Huger had thought Lafayette's men were Hessians who had deserted the British army. For days, the Hessians had been stumbling upon his property from out of the forest. Major Huger was a patriot officer and he greeted Lafayette and his party warmly after the mix-up, despite their entirely unexpected arrival.

For a few weeks, Lafayette and his party stayed in the area around Charleston. Here their host and the locals treated them quite well. Finally the group had enjoyed the local culture long enough and Lafayette decided to begin the eight-hundred-mile (1,288-km) journey north to Philadelphia. In Philadelphia, they would inform Congress that they were ready to serve in the Continental army. They had letters from Silas Deane explaining who they were and what they had been promised in terms of rank.

There were few roads or inns at this time so the group's journey was quite difficult. It was brutally hot that summer and they were forced to travel through many swamps and thick forests. It seemed mosquitoes attacked them during the entire trip. Despite the problems, Lafayette's spirits were good. He wrote to

Adrienne, "The farther north I go, the more I like this country and its inhabitants. I've had nothing but courtesy and kindness although many hardly know who I am."

On July 27, 1777, Lafayette's group arrived in Philadelphia. They brushed off their uniforms and within two hours were in the Congress building. James Lovell, president of the Committee of Foreign Affairs, heard their request to serve in the American army and took their letters of recommendation from Deane. Lovell left the room, telling them to return tomorrow at the same time. Lafayette said, "It was more like a dismissal than a welcome." Indeed, the following day, Lovell informed the group that they would not be serving in the American army. They were told that their services were not needed and that they should return to France. Lafayette and his group were stunned. Congress was opposed to granting any more commissions to foreign officers. Silas Deane had been sending greedy adventurers and conceited officers from France and the Americans were rightfully upset. Congress felt that only American soldiers who had proven themselves in battle should be promoted and made officers.

Lafayette was not about to return to France after what he had gone through to come to America. He wrote to the president of Congress, John Hancock, offering to serve as a volunteer without pay. "After the sacrifices that I have made in this cause, I have the right to ask two favors at your hands: The one is, to serve without pay at

John Hancock was born on January 23, 1737, in Braintree (now Quincy), Massachusetts. After graduating from Harvard in 1754, Hancock joined his uncle's firm, and ten years later he took over, becoming the wealthiest merchant in New England. He joined the protest against the Stamp Act because British taxation impacted his business. He was elected the president of the Continental Congress and made his famous signature on the Declaration of Independence. He died on October 8, 1793.

my own expense; and the other, that I be allowed to serve at first as a volunteer in the ranks." He also called on his American connections, primarily Benjamin Franklin, who ensured that Lafayette would stay.

Congress eventually decided that someone of Lafayette's stature in France should not be brushed off and someone of DeKalb's confirmed qualifications was rare. On July 31, the Continental Congress gave Lafayette his appointment as major general. Lafayette would get his rank, but General George Washington would determine when Lafayette would get his own unit to lead. All of the others in Lafayette's party were dismissed except for Baron DeKalb, who would also serve in the Continental army.

The following day, Lafayette met with George Washington for the first time. Lafayette was impressed with Washington immediately. Washington was tall and carried himself well. Although Washington was a bit shocked at Lafayette's youth and poor command of the English language, he admired Lafayette for traveling so far to fight for the colonists. As time went by, a friendship developed between the two that would last as long as Washington lived. At the end of their meeting, Lafayette was invited by Washington to stay at his headquarters where he made friends with other members of Washington's staff before joining the troops.

Lafayette's first experience with the Continental army was shocking to him. The fall of 1777 was a bad

This Currier & Ives lithograph shows the first meeting of George Washington and Marquis de Lafayette in early August 1777. The two men would become good friends over time. In fact, George Washington often called Lafayette "My dear Marquis" in letters.

time for the American soldiers. Poorly funded by Congress, the army did not have enough supplies or clothing. Lafayette joined the army in Pennsylvania at the Neshaminy encampment. His first impression was that there were "about 11,000 men, poorly armed and worse dressed . . . often naked." Of those lucky enough to be wearing clothing, many were wearing British uniforms they had stripped from the dead. They were also poorly trained and could not even perform the simplest military commands without error. In spite of this,

Lafayette was optimistic about his assignment and wrote Washington constantly requesting his own regiment. Washington regularly ignored his requests. He still did not know Lafayette very well and Lafayette had yet to prove himself.

The first major battle that Lafayette would participate in was the Battle of Brandywine, fought on September 11, 1777. Washington had hoped to prevent a large group of British troops from crossing Brandywine Creek. During this battle, Washington was continually moving his troops and unable to make a well-planned attack. He

This painting of the 1777 battle of Brandywine, near Chadds Ford, Pennsylvania, is by F. C. Yohns. The British forces, in red above, numbered about 18,000, and the Americans, dressed in blue, had 11,000 men. Nine hundred Americans were killed or wounded and 400 were taken prisoner. The British casualties totaled 600 men.

kept receiving conflicting reports about where the British planned on crossing the creek and kept delaying the strike. Many troops began to retreat against orders. Sir William Howe, leading the British, had outmaneuvered the Continental army and was crossing the creek north of where Washington and his troops were stationed. Howe crossed the creek and then had his troops move south to attack. American officers were pushing, shouting, and bullying their troops so that they would hold their position. Realizing he must do something to inspire the troops, Lafayette himself went to the front line. He tried to persuade the troops to stay and in doing so put himself in great danger. British sharpshooters took aim at his brightly colored general's uniform and Lafayette was shot through the leg, below his left calf. He continued to lead his troops and shout encouragement until blood from his wound filled up his boot and began pouring over the top of it. Low on ammunition, Washington was eventually forced to retreat. Lafayette refused to dismount from his horse until his troops found shelter twelve miles (19 km) from the field of battle. Only then would he receive much-needed medical attention.

Lafayette had displayed bravery in his first battle, but Brandywine was a terrible defeat for American forces. More than 1,300 men were killed, captured, or wounded. For the British, 89 were dead, 480 were wounded, and 6 were missing. Lafayette, even in defeat, had gained a great deal of respect from his troops for his passion and bravery. He'd led from the front, unlike most generals who did not want to put themselves in the line of enemy fire. Lafayette also refused to leave the battlefield even after he was shot.

After Brandywine, Washington moved his troops to Valley Forge, Pennsylvania, to prepare for the long winter ahead. Lafayette, despite his wound, had gotten a taste of action and loved it. He wrote a letter to Adrienne while recovering from a badly swollen leg that pained him. Lafayette, making light of a serious injury, wrote to Adrienne that he received "only a little wound in the leg, but it's nothing my dear heart, the ball touched neither bone, nor nerve," and that he looked forward to his next battle. Washington, after seeing Lafayette's bravery first-hand, took a liking to the young Frenchman. He even sent his own medical attendant to tend to Lafayette's wound and instructed him to treat Lafayette as his son, not just his friend.

Back home in France, Adrienne gave birth to another girl, Anastasie, on July 1, 1777. As Lafayette recovered, he continued to request his own group to command. His wound healed slowly and though he longed to return to battle he spent a great deal of time in bed. After three months, Lafayette insisted on returning to the Continental army. When Lafayette returned to service, he was still limping and was unable to wear a boot on his wounded leg. Upon reaching camp again, he was viewed with great respect and was praised almost unanimously by his fellow officers and soldiers.

In November 1777, after returning to active service, Lafayette would be victorious in a raid on a group of Hessians in New Jersey. Lafayette and three hundred Continental soldiers had stumbled across a group of 350 Hessians by chance. Though outnumbered, Lafayette's men waited patiently for a good time to strike. When they did, they struck hard, killing and scattering the entire group. Although it was a small victory, any battle won by colonial troops did a great deal for the army's morale. Sixty British had been killed, wounded, or captured, while only one American officer was felled, and five were wounded.

During the winter at Valley Forge, anti-Washington feelings developed among some of the officers and soldiers. Several officers wanted to relieve him of his command of the Continental army. They gained some support and then approached Lafayette for his support, as well. Lafayette informed them that he would not even listen to such absurd talk. Washington was the man who would lead the Continental army to victory.

Lafayette wrote a letter to Washington explaining the situation and told him how loyal he was to the general. Washington responded to Lafayette's letter and let him know how much his support meant. Eventually the group that wanted to overthrow Washington fell apart. There were too many people loyal to the general and not enough that wanted him forced out of his position.

5. Lafayette Receives His Own Regiment

On December 1, 1777, Washington informed Congress that Lafayette was worthy of his own regiment, "In recognition of the military talents of which he has just given brilliant evidence." Lafayette was only twenty years old and he had earned the respect of the man he most admired. In honor of Washington, whose home was in Virginia, Lafayette chose to lead a group of Virginians. He was now in a position to gain the military glory he had wanted for so long. Lafayette, widely known as Washington's friend, became very popular in America. He captured the hearts of Americans and many stories were written about him in newspapers and pamphlets.

When Lafayette first met his troops, he saw how poorly they were dressed. Some wore nothing at all. This was not acceptable. He immediately purchased clothing and supplies with his own money and began training them for a spring offensive against the British. Despite being young and inexperienced, Lafayette's early problems as commander were the same that any other commander would have. He had to figure out ways to get supplies, food, and salaries for his troops when none of these things were easy to obtain.

Spending the winter camped at Valley Forge was worse for the Americans than any battle they had lost so far. They had little, if any, food, clothing, or shelter. Medical attention was not sufficient and many men had limbs amputated because of frostbite. Many were dying. Washington rightly feared a mutiny or mass desertion. Deserters would often turn up on the doorsteps of civilians. The deserters were in such poor shape that they

This engraving shows George Washington meeting with Marquis de Lafayette at Valley Forge. The winter at Valley Forge was a harsh one for the American troops. Men were starving and freezing to death. Many soldiers chose to desert the army during this winter. Washington was proud of the men who chose to remain. He believed their willingness to deal with such hard times for the American cause proved the righteousness of their fight for independence from Britain.

were not reported because the residents felt so bad for them. In all, the number of soldiers at Valley Forge fell from seventeen thousand to five thousand during the winter because of death and desertion. Those troops that did stay proved Washington's belief in their spirit and dedication to the American cause. Washington said, "To see the men without clothes to cover their nakedness, without blankets to lie upon, without shoes . . . is a proof of patience and obedience, which, in my opinion can scarcely be paralleled."

Early in 1778, in spite of the problems at Valley Forge, there was some optimism in America. The British were not as powerful as they seemed. Their supply lines from Europe were not very reliable and their war effort was unorganized. More good news was to come for the Americans.

On February 6, 1778, two treaties were signed in France. One recognized America as an independent nation and the other announced her as a loyal ally of France. Neither nation would make a truce with Britain without the other agreeing to the terms. When news of the treaties reached America three months later, there was a lot of celebrating. Unfortunately for Lafayette, at this time he would also learn of the death of his first daughter, Henriette, from illness.

American general Horatio Gates was never a big supporter of Washington and wanted to strip him of his power. He began to come up with a plot to do this. Gates

This is an engraved portrait of American general Horatio Gates, who lived from 1728 to 1806. Gates was an excellent general and was in charge of one of the most important colonial victories of the American Revolution, the defeat of Burgoyne at Saratoga. He was viewed as a serious rival of George Washington, but the Conway Cabal, started with the aim of making Gates commander in chief instead of Washington, failed when Gates himself wrote in defense of Washington.

himself was very powerful in America and he convinced Congress to appoint a Board of War over which Gates would have control. Gates suggested a Canadian invasion, saying it would be very important to attack the British in the north. Gates requested Lafayette to lead the assault. Secretly, Gates knew it would be an operation that would fail and also one that would put Lafayette at great risk. He hoped to break up the team of Lafayette and Washington, realizing they were a very strong alliance when together. Washington was notified of the board's decision and told that Lafayette was needed to lead the invasion of Canada.

The Board of War promised Lafayette three thousand men and unlimited supplies. Washington agreed to send Lafayette north, but Lafayette did not want to go. Washington, sensing something was not right with the plans, even told Lafayette that the invasion would likely not happen, but that he should go anyway. Lafayette went to York and then to Albany, where he met Governor George Clinton, another supporter of George Washington. Clinton was not in favor of the attack, either. Clinton then found out that Generals Philip Schuyler, Benjamin Lincoln, and Benedict Arnold all opposed the expedition because of a lack of money, supplies, and manpower. The generals were disgusted by Gates and the actions of the Board of War. The attack was sure to fail because Canada already knew details of the proposed invasion and was prepared in case of attack. When Congress found out that the Board of War had planned to attack in winter, they were stunned. With few troops and little clothing and supplies, an attack on Canada in winter would be suicide. Finally Congress sent letters to Lafayette delaying the expedition, and in March 1778, Congress scrapped plans of the attack for good. In April Lafayette returned to Valley Forge, where Washington warmly welcomed his friend back to his side.

By now, George Washington trusted Lafayette a great deal. Washington had just learned that the British stationed at Barren Hill in Philadelphia were about to move. Lafayette was sent with two thousand men to obtain more details of their planned departure. Unfortunately, a British spy informed the enemy that Lafayette was coming. A large British force was sent to surround Lafayette and his men. Luckily for him, the colonists captured two British soldiers and learned of the trap in time. Recalling that Washington said intelligence and not bravery was the most important thing during wartime, Lafayette thought of a way to retreat safely. He knew of a lower road where he could hide his troops as they withdrew. The British were left empty-handed and frustrated.

After their trap for Lafayette failed, the British proceeded with their plan to move from Philadelphia. Sir Henry Clinton started moving most of his fifteen thousand British troops and fifteen hundred wagons of supplies by foot through New Jersey to New York. The rest

This portrait by F. C. Yohn shows General George Washington during the American Revolution on a horse. George Washington is one of the most-painted people of all time. In this painting, Washington is in uniform and is pointing as though giving orders to his troops.

would sail the Delaware River. Washington and Lafayette followed, along with General Charles Lee, whom they met along the way.

Before British officer Clinton could reach New York, Washington engaged the British in the Battle of Monmouth on June 28, 1778. Washington had decided to force a confrontation in the hopes of preventing the British from reaching New York. During the battle, communication between Generals Lee, Washington, and Lafayette was very poor. There was major confusion and conflicting reports on where the British troops were, how many there were, and where they planned to attack. Washington ordered an attack, but when he arrived, he saw Lee retreating. Lee wanted glory, but he retreated when he saw the risk involved. Lafayette and Washington stopped the retreat, reorganized the men, and led the attack. In the end, the British continued north as they had hoped, but they had suffered unexpected losses, including six hundred deserters. The Americans, exhausted from the ninety-five-degree heat that day, were too tired to pursue in the end. It was the longest battle of the war thus far. Lee was harshly criticized by Washington and Lafayette for his lack of leadership and would be found guilty of disobedience. Lafayette, although not heroic, managed to keep his troops together during a bad situation and won even more respect from Washington.

Despite the success he encountered on the battle-

This is an engraving of the Battle of Monmouth, fought near the Monmouth Courthouse in Freehold, New Jersey, on June 28, 1778. Though the battle was basically a draw, there were more British casualties than American deaths. The American people viewed it as a victory and it boosted the morale of the troops and public support of the war.

field, Lafayette began to think he could help the American cause more by returning to France. By going in person to the king, he felt he could persuade the French government to plan a major attack against the British in either England or Canada. Of course, he felt he should lead this campaign when it came about.

On October 29, 1778, Congress passed a resolution permitting Lafayette to leave America and return to France. They sent Louis XVI a letter praising Lafayette's service and provided a ship for his journey home. Before

This painting shows the legendary Molly Pitcher helping to load a cannon during the Battle of Monmouth.

The legend of Molly Pitcher comes from the Battle of Monmouth. During the battle, Mary Ludwig brought water to American soldiers to drink as they fought in the very hot weather. Water also cooled the cannons. Legend has it that when her husband, a gunner, collapsed from the heat, she took the gun herself and began firing on the British. History has given her the nickname Molly Pitcher.

he left, Lafayette spent a great deal of time consulting with Washington on how best to use the aid that France was supplying. He was also waiting in the hopes of leading a properly funded Canadian invasion that would bring him glory. The Canadian invasion did not happen and on January 11, 1779, the time had come for Lafayette to return to France. Before leaving he wrote one last note to Washington, "I hope I shall see you soon again, and tell you myself with what emotion I now leave the coast you inhabit, and with what affection and respect. I am forever, my dear general, your respectful and sincere friend."

Once again, Lafayette had an eventful trip across the ocean. Any long ocean trip at this time carried the threat of pirates, worry about a lack of supplies, and improper medical care. On this trip, Lafayette suffered terrible seasickness once again. He also thought that he would die when a terrible storm almost sank the ship. Then, just a few hundred miles (km) from French shores, a near mutiny occurred. Fortunately for Lafayette and the crew, a betrayer told the ship's officers of the plan. Those involved in the plot were bound in irons until the ship safely reached France.

Lafayette arrived at the port of Brest in northwest France on February 6, 1779. He went to Versailles to report about the war effort before even seeing his family. Because he had left without permission, he needed to be forgiven by the king. As punishment, Louis XVI placed him under house arrest for a week in the Noailles mansion where only his family could visit him. It was not much of a punishment at all. It gave Lafayette a chance to spend time with his wife and family. He was very happy to see Adrienne again and to learn that she had given birth to another daughter, Anastasie, but he was also saddened by the death of his first daughter Henriette. Once his exile ended, both the king and queen received Lafayette very graciously. He was glorified as The Hero of the New World and many dinners and functions were given in his honor. Benjamin Franklin's grandson would present the Marquis with a beautiful sword from Congress. The sword was engraved with his coat of arms and with something representing each of the military actions in which Lafayette had taken part.

For many months after his return to France, Lafayette unsuccessfully campaigned for a French invasion of England. As he waited for France to plan her next move, he spent a lot of time with the people he had missed while he was away. On December 24, 1779, Adrienne gave birth to a son. He was named Georges Washington de Lafayette in honor of the American general. General Washington would also be named the young boy's godfather.

Although France was still reluctant to participate in an all-out attack on the British, in 1780, France did agree to provide more assistance to the colonists. France would continue to help until the Americans had enough supplies

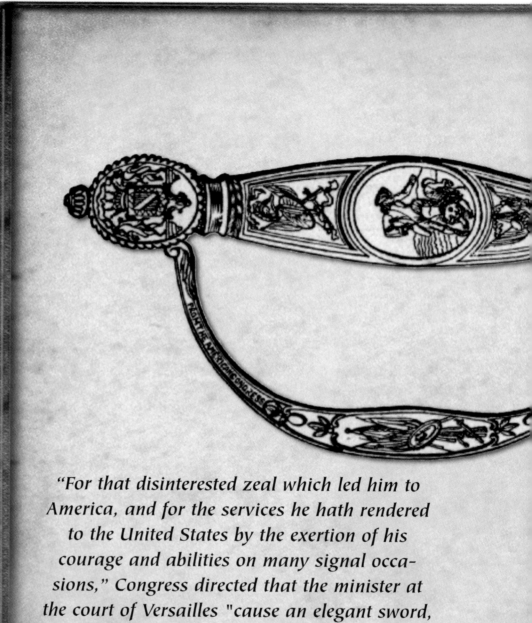

"For that disinterested zeal which led him to America, and for the services he hath rendered to the United States by the exertion of his courage and abilities on many signal occasions," Congress directed that the minister at the court of Versailles "cause an elegant sword, with proper devices, to be made and presented"

to Lafayette in the name of the United States.
Benjamin Franklin's grandson presented the
Marquis with this beautiful sword from
Congress. The sword was engraved with his coat
of arms and with scenes representing each of the
military actions in which Lafayette had taken
part, before he returned to France in 1779.

and manpower to win the war. The French sent six ships under Admiral de Termay and six thousand men with the Count de Rochambeau. Lafayette was directed to go back to America to help once again. This time he would go as an official representative of Louis XVI. Lafayette was happy to be returning to America but at the same time he was very disappointed. He had been in France for a whole year and had not even led a skirmish as the head of French troops against the British in Europe.

6. Lafayette Returns to America

Lafayette arrived in Boston on April 28, 1780. Although few knew he was coming, when the Americans found out Lafayette had arrived, he got a hero's welcome from the people of Massachusetts. In early April, Washington, who was not an emotional man, reacted with tears when he read Lafayette's letter informing him that the Marquis would be returning. Unknown when he first arrived on the shores of South Carolina three years before, Lafayette was returning to America as a hero.

During his second tour with the American army, Lafayette was put in charge of the Light Division. The Light Division was made up of twenty-three hundred Virginia men whom, once again, Lafayette clothed at his own expense. He drilled them over and over in preparation for battle until they had become one of the best units in the Continental army.

There was little fighting going on in 1780, and those battles that were fought went poorly for the Americans. In May, General Benjamin Lincoln surrendered Charleston, South Carolina, to the British.

British general Sir Banastre Tarleton's cavalry destroyed a Virginia regiment at Waxhaw and in August, General Lord Charles Cornwallis badly beat General Horatio Gates at Camden where Lafayette's old friend DeKalb was killed.

In early 1781, Lafayette was sent by Washington to pursue Benedict Arnold in Virginia. Arnold had been an American general but had turned over important documents to the British. In return, the British made him a general in charge of two thousand men. Lafayette was sent south where a joint American and French force would attack Arnold by land and sea. Lafayette, although successful in harassing Arnold and his troops, never captured him.

Because Lafayette and his troops were now in the south, Washington instructed him to aid General Nathanael Greene in his fight against Cornwallis. General Greene had just one-fifth the number of troops that Cornwallis had. Even though most of Lafayette's troops wished to return north, Lafayette and his troops were desperately needed to help Greene. Lafayette arrived in Richmond, Virginia, just before Cornwallis captured it.

Although the Americans were still outnumbered, Lafayette did just enough to keep Cornwallis occupied. He regularly engaged in small skirmishes with Cornwallis, harassing him just enough to prevent his escape to North or South Carolina. Washington and

Benedict Arnold's legacy in America is that he will forever be known as a traitor. Arnold was a patriot officer who was a successful general for four years in the Continental army. At one point, he was passed over for a promotion to major general, which was given to a younger officer instead. Later, after marrying a woman who was very sympathetic to the British, Arnold began giving American information to the British. Eventually he stole important American documents and in return was awarded a British generalship. At the end of 1781, after escaping capture by the Continental army, he went to England, where he would remain the rest of his life.

French general, Sean-Baptiste Rochambeau hoped to arrive soon with six thousand men and a large portion of the French fleet. It was very important for Lafayette to prevent Cornwallis from establishing stronger British control in the south. Despite the lack of men and supplies, Lafayette did a great job avoiding capture until reinforcements arrived. In June, General "Mad" Anthony Wayne arrived with five hundred men to aid Lafayette and Greene. Frustrated at being unable to capture Lafayette or even defeat him decisively, Cornwallis chose to move his troops north.

Cornwallis began to move his troops to Yorktown, where he would set up camp on the York River in Virginia. His orders were to retain a naval base on the Chesapeake that could be used in a future British attack on Philadelphia. Cornwallis also thought that Governor Clinton would send ships from New York to help him if he were stationed in Yorktown.

Lafayette advanced slowly as Cornwallis had his troops fortify themselves in Yorktown. The British were confident that if they waited a bit longer, reinforcements would arrive or they'd be able to escape by sea. Cornwallis was wrong. In moving his troops north, he had made a huge error. Lafayette wrote to Washington saying the British forces could be trapped on the peninsula at Yorktown if the American troops could be brought together quickly. Washington immediately made plans to move his troops there for the attack.

On August 21, 1781, Washington began marching to Virginia to join Lafayette. After a successful battle with the British navy, French admiral de Grasse was also on his way into the area with twenty-four warships and three thousand men. They landed on September 5, 1781, and joined Marquis de Lafayette's troops in Williamsburg, Virginia. On September 14, Washington arrived at the camp, and the rest of the American and French forces were there within ten days.

On September 28, 1781, Washington ordered the soldiers to advance on Yorktown where General Cornwallis was barricaded. Once there, they set up camp. On October 6, the American troops began to dig trenches that would

Lafayette, while fighting for America, had a slave to assist him, named James. James had volunteered his service to the American cause. Lafayette often used James as a spy. James would pose as a black runaway and would cross into enemy territory to get information, then would report back to Lafayette. James did such a good job that Lafayette wrote a certificate praising his service. After the war, James used Lafayette's letter to request his freedom. James, like most slaves, had no last name in English. After the war, he gained his freedom and adopted the last name Lafayette, which he would use for life.

get them closer to their target without exposing them to British fire, and on October 9, an assault was possible. The honor of leading the first four hundred Americans into battle was given to Lafayette. It would be Lafayette's biggest chance at glory on the battlefield. Realizing the importance of the battle, Washington even gave a short inspirational speech to Lafayette's troops before the attack. The Americans opened fire and the Battle of Yorktown began. On October 14, the colonists captured two major redoubts, putting the British in serious trouble. Three days later, Cornwallis requested a cease-fire, but he was refused. Only unconditional surrender would be accepted. On October 19, 1781, more than eight thousand Hessians and British troops officially surrendered to Washington. An American flag was raised in victory.

Although there were still more skirmishes fought after Yorktown, and an official treaty had not been signed yet, the Americans had won the Revolutionary War. Lafayette, the young French major general, had played an important part in the crucial battle that secured victory for the Americans.

Soon after Lafayette wrote to the French prime minister, informing him the war was over and that the British would likely sign a treaty within two years. Plans were made for Lafayette to return home to France to raise more aid and enthusiasm for the American cause. On Christmas Day 1781, after saying farewell to Washington and other French officers, he left America on board the *Alliance*. Upon his departure, George Washington wrote to Lafayette:

> *"I owe it to your friendship and to my affectionate regard to you my dear Marquis, not to let you leave this country without you carrying with you, fresh marks of my attachment to you, and new expressions of the high sense I entertain of your military conduct and other important services in the course of the last campaign."*

Lafayette responded:

> *"Adieu my dear general; I know your heart so well that I am sure that no distance can alter your attachment to me . . . at the moment of leaving you, I felt more than ever the strength of those friendly ties that forever bind me to you."*

7. Trouble in France

Lafayette returned home to cheering crowds in France in early 1782, and the king and queen showered him with medals. Lafayette was seen everywhere throughout France. He entertained and was entertained by all the important members of society. Lafayette had played a vital role in the greatest victory in the Revolutionary War so far and had done much to strengthen ties between France and the United States.

Adrienne had another girl in September 1782. They named her Virginie. After Virginie's birth, doctors advised Adrienne not to have any more children. Lafayette then moved his wife and three children into a mansion on Rue de Bourbon.

In January 1783, Lafayette was involved in planning a French attack on the British West Indies when a preliminary treaty was signed between the United States and Britain. The attack was canceled. France's help was no longer needed.

In America, the war was over and the United States finally had its independence. Washington retired after the war and moved to Mount Vernon. In 1784, Washington invited Lafayette to come for an extended visit. Lafayette spent two weeks in Mount Vernon with Washington and four months in America. He made many speeches throughout the United States about the need for a strong federal government. All the honors generally given to great men were given to the twenty-seven-year-old Lafayette. Every village named a street after him and every male in his family was given hereditary citizenship in the union. He received many awards and was treated well, but shortly after arriving he began to get homesick. He realized that all the action in America was political and was no longer military. Lafayette missed the excitement of fighting or preparing for battles. In January 1785, he went home. Once back in France, he still continued to help America when needed. During the years that followed, Lafayette would aid Thomas Jefferson, U.S. minister to France, on numerous political and economic matters.

In 1785, the political situation in France was very unstable. The relationship was terrible between the government and the people. The government ruled without regard for the people. There were constant demonstrations by citizens throughout France. In 1789, the people were ready to revolt. Most of the people were so poor in Paris that they could not even afford bread. People were screaming for the king to do something to help them and riots were breaking out everywhere.

With all the problems in France, Lafayette was hopeful the situation would bring about major changes in the French government. Because the people were so unhappy, he felt that the ruling parties would have to change the way they governed the people. With the help of Thomas Jefferson and using the Bill of Rights as a guide, Lafayette started working on a document that he hoped would serve as a basis for a new French government. When Lafayette addressed the existing government on July 11, he suggested that the people should have a voice in government affairs. He presented to the assembly the "Declaration of the Rights of Man and Citizen." This was, he hoped, a model of how France should govern. Initially, the assembly and aristocrats thought the document was ridiculous. They made fun of Lafayette for even suggesting that the people should have a voice in government. The queen even accused him of being "a traitor to his class."

The French people demanded to be heard. They refused to let the monarchy continue to govern as it had in the past. On July 14, 1789, sixty thousand angry Parisans marched on the Bastille prison, hanging and beheading officials along the way. There were actually more armed citizens than soldiers in Paris on this day. The aristocracy feared for their lives and felt that only Lafayette would be able to control the people. On July 15, King Louis XVI named Lafayette commander of the National Guard. After getting the position, Lafayette immediately tried to restore order. Speaking against the revolt, he promised he would convince the government to

This hand-colored engraving shows the attack on the Bastille on July 14, 1789. The French Revolution was reaching a boiling point and Lafayette was called upon to restore order. He promised that he would convince the government to give more power to the people.

give more power to the people. It has been said that Lafayette was the one who was truly in power in France at this time.

Louis XVI was forced to obey the will of the majority after seeing the riots at the Bastille. Using the "Declaration of the Rights of Man and Citizen" as a model, the French government began their first attempt at reform. The people, however, felt the government was not working fast enough. On October 5, 1789, more than fifty thousand people marched on Versailles demanding that Louis XVI agree to the abolition of feudal privileges and adopt Lafayette's

This hand-colored print shows Lafayette as commander of the French National Guard. The National Guard was formed to protect the city from outside forces as well as the real possibility of destruction by its own people. The guardsmen were sympathetic to the people but, on July 17, 1791, were forced to fire into the crowd to maintain order.

"Declaration of the Rights of Man and Citizen." The crowds refused to disperse and Lafayette was forced to appear with the king and queen to restore calm and save them from the fury of the mob. Lafayette needed to reconcile the people with the monarchy's body-guards. To do this, he took a small tricolor ribbon from his own cap and put it on the white cockade of a body-guard, then embraced him. White was always a symbol of the monarchy, and red and blue were the colors of Paris. The tricolor symbolized unity between the monarchy and the people of France. The people cheered Lafayette's gesture and dispersed soon after.

For the next year, Lafayette was at the height of his

This is an eighteenth-century color print of the march to Versailles that occurred on October 5, 1789. Notice that there are both men and women in the crowd, all bearing weapons. Once again, Lafayette was called upon to restore order and to save the life of the king and queen.

Lafayette created the French national flag, the tricolor. In France, white always symbolized the color of the monarchy. During the revolt of 1789, Lafayette pinned the white to the blue and red colors associated with the city of Paris, and the tricolor flag was born. Lafayette had pinned them together to promote unity between the monarchy and the people. A law was passed on February 15, 1794, establishing the tricolor as the national flag. Today, it flies on all public buildings in France.

influence and popularity. He supported measures to transfer some power from the aristocracy to the people, but after being granted some power, the people wanted more. Soon, republicans did not want a constitutional monarchy at all. A crowd gathered on July 17, 1791, and demanded that the king abdicate. Lafayette, leader of the National Guard, was forced to have his guards open fire on the group. More than forty people were killed or wounded and Lafayette would see his popularity greatly affected.

Lafayette was now the master of three forces: king, assembly, and people. All were suspicious of each other and all went to Versailles in 1789 to make sure they would be governing France in the years to come. Lafayette was in an impossible situation. Many believed he had no loyalty to either the people or the monarchy. They felt he was simply trying to boost his own image. The government felt that he identified too much with the people, and the people did not think he supported them as much as he should. The people felt that Lafayette was afraid of losing his power in government. Once beloved, Lafayette was beginning to be hated in many parts of his homeland.

Eventually, under constant verbal harassment and threats, Louis XVI and the royal family attempted to flee to Austria. Louis XVI was soon captured and was brought back to France. Moderate members of government had written a document that would save the monarchy but also would give power to the people. Louis XVI accepted it on September 14, 1791.

In spite of these problems, all parties were attempting to reach a compromise. During this unsettling time in government, numerous political groups came about, including the Jacobins. The Jacobins began as any other political group had—trying to get followers and to make their voice heard. This would change, as their ideas on reforming the government became more and more severe. The Jacobins split in 1791, because moderate members did not want to forcefully remove the king. Those radicals who remained were led by Maximilien Robespierre.

Lafayette was constantly being criticized in Jacobin papers during this time. Unfortunately, the French people seemed to believe anything that was written. On October 1, the National Assembly was dissolved and a week later Lafayette retired his post as commander of the Paris National Guard and went home to Auvergne.

Lafayette tried to relax, but shortly thereafter he was called back into service. France had gone to war with Austria on April 20, 1792. Almost immediately Louis XVI began to lose power and the confidence of the people. On August 10, the monarchy was forcefully overthrown and the Jacobins took control. They began executing large numbers of people with the use of a new invention called the guillotine. Aristocrats began to leave France, fearing for their lives. While hiding in

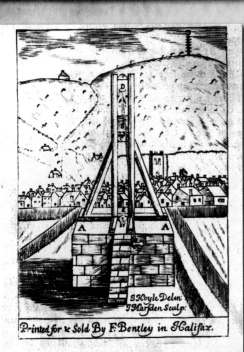

A A. The Scaffold.
B. The piece of wood wherein the Axe is fix'd.
C. The Axe.
D. The Pulley by which the Axe is drawn up.
E. The Malefactor who lyes to be beheaded.
F. The pin to which the Rope is ty'd that draws up the Axe.

The guillotine was not named for the person who invented it, as nobody knows who actually invented it. We do know for whom it was named, though. Dr. Guillotin was the person who lobbied the French government for a more "merciful" way to execute people, because many other execution techniques of the time were slower and more painful. The guillotine was a board to which the victim was tied. A hole was cut in the board where the victim's head went. A sharp blade was then dropped onto the person's neck and the victim's head would fall into a basket. In all, twenty-five hundred people were guillotined during the French Revolution.

neighboring countries, they tried to convince foreign leaders to declare war on France to halt the spread of such radical ideas.

Lafayette was impeached during the rise of the Jacobin influence. Extreme members of the assembly took over and had Lafayette's properties confiscated, also ordering his arrest. Lafayette attempted to flee to Belgium. From there, he planned to set sail for the United States until the trouble passed. Unfortunately Belgium in 1792 was part of the Austrian Netherlands and was at war with France. Lafayette was captured, arrested, and taken to Francis II, the Holy Roman Emperor. The emperor felt that Lafayette was a republican and therefore was against monarchies, so he sentenced him to life in prison. Shortly after Lafayette fled to Belgium, Adrienne was arrested in France. On December 24, 1792, she was released on parole so she could take care of her children.

In early 1793, the Reign of Terror began. The Committee of Public Safety, led by Robespierre, had nearly complete control over France. Anyone against the Revolution and the committee

This cartoon depicts the execution of Louis XVI. The original caption read: "The Apogee of Freedom. Cartoon against the French Revolution and the execution of Louis XVI, 1793."

went to the guillotine. In January 1793, Louis XVI was beheaded. Shortly after, the queen, Marie Antoinette, shared the same fate. Both aristocrats and moderates were regularly executed. In all, three hundred thousand suspects were arrested and countless were executed. The Reign of Terror ended when a more moderate group overpowered the Jacobins and sent Robespierre himself to the guillotine on July 27, 1794.

In November 1793, Adrienne had been imprisoned again and during the summer of 1794, Adrienne's grandmother, mother, and sister were killed during the Reign of Terror. Sadly, Adrienne's family was executed only five days before a moderate group came to power in France. Under Jacobin rule, Adrienne had feared for her life daily. Soon after the Jacobins were overthrown, the American ambassador to France, James Monroe, helped negotiate her freedom. She was released on January 21, 1795.

After his arrest, Lafayette was sent to a Prussian fortress in Westphalia. He was transferred several times to other prisons in Germany before winding up at Olmutz in Austria. During Lafayette's prison stay, George Washington wrote many letters to gain Lafayette's release but they all went unanswered. At this time very few people even knew in which prison he was being kept.

During his many years in prison, Lafayette attempted to escape only once. A group of Americans

This 1768 oil painting of Archduchess Marie Antoinette is by the
Master of the Archduchesses, whose name is unknown. The painting
shows Marie Antoinette at age twelve, while she was still living with her
family in Austria. In 1770, at age fourteen, Marie Antoinette left Austria
and traveled to the French palace of Versailles to marry Louis XVI.

had hired Erich Bollman, a German adventurer, to help free him in 1794. By chance, while working on an escape plan for Lafayette, Bollman met Francis Kinlock Huger, who was studying medicine at the University of Vienna. Francis Huger was the son of Major Huger, whose home Lafayette had stumbled upon when he first arrived in South Carolina twenty years earlier. After learning of Lafayette's situation, Huger was determined to help. On November 8, 1794, while on his usual walk, Lafayette received assistance from a bribed jailer and left his holding area to meet with Huger and Bollman. Huger, Bollman, and Lafayette were forced to fight with prison guards to ensure his escape via horseback. Though Lafayette made it off prison grounds, his escape was short-lived. He was separated from Bollman and Huger and recaptured the next day. He was sentenced to six months of solitary confinement during which time he was not allowed to write anyone or exercise at all. Huger and Bollman were jailed for a year but then were released.

Lafayette's family missed him terribly and constantly worried about his health. After being released from prison herself, Adrienne went to Austria to beg for his release. When Holy Roman Emperor Francis II refused to release him, Adrienne and her two daughters offered to join Lafayette in prison at Olmutz.

On October 15, 1795, they got their wish. Emperor Francis II even said, "You are quite right. In your place,

This E. Henne engraving, after a drawing by P. C. D'Agrain, is called
Captiere de La Fayette, which translates to "the Imprisonment of
Lafayette." The engraving shows the final two years of his imprison-
ment, when Adrienne and Lafayette's daughters have joined him.

I should have done just as you are doing." Lafayette's son, Georges Washington, was sent to America and Adrienne, Anastasie, and Virginie joined Lafayette in his cell. They did not want him to endure his sentence alone. By joining him, they also hoped to make the public more aware of how unjust his imprisonment was.

Peace negotiations between France and Austria began in April 1797. Napoleon Bonaparte had become a huge success as a leader of the French military and won major victories over Austria in the war. Napoleon hoped to become ruler of France and the public in France felt that Napoleon should be active in helping Lafayette and his family gain their release from prison. With Napoleon's help and that of the United States, Lafayette's release was finally negotiated. On September 19, 1797, the family was set free. Adrienne was very sick the whole time she was with Lafayette in prison. Once released from prison, she battled a terrible case of scurvy and would never truly recover.

8. The Napoleonic Era

Lafayette was now a free man again, but he was forty years old and unsure of what to do. He had spent five and a half years in prison. The Directory, the moderate group in power in France, had helped to negotiate his release. They had agreed to do so only if he promised not to return to France. They feared he would stir up the people against the government. Lafayette, now poor and unemployed, thought about going to America. Adrienne, however, was too sick to make the journey. Also, there was friction between the two countries that were once allies. In the end, the family settled in Holland for a while.

Lafayette stayed in Holland for two years, as Adrienne attempted to recover her health. He was happy and rested during this time even though he still hoped to return to France. The government knew Adrienne was not the threat her husband was. As her health slowly improved, Adrienne was allowed into France. She would go for visits and then return to Holland to tell Lafayette what was happening in their homeland.

In late 1799, Adrienne convinced him the time was right to return. Lafayette returned to France only to find his fortune destroyed and the French government still in turmoil. Claiming he was devoted to the people, Napoleon had overthrown the Directory on November 9, 1799. Napoleon was then head of a three-person consulate in which he was first consul and, technically, in command. Napoleon, unfortunately, was not nearly the success in government that he had been on the battlefield.

Lafayette mistakenly thought that Napoleon would want him to take over his old position as commander of the National Guard when he returned to France. Napoleon, however, ignored Lafayette's presence and told him to live his life out of the public eye. Napoleon did not want to compete with Lafayette for popularity, so Lafayette moved to his home at LaGrange where he hoped to have some peace.

On December 14, 1799, George Washington died. Washington and Lafayette had maintained almost a father-son relationship since they had met and Lafayette was heartbroken when he learned of Washington's death. Napoleon did not invite Lafayette to the French memorial service for Washington. In fact, despite how much Lafayette and Washington had been through together, Lafayette's name was not even mentioned during the service.

Napoleon and Lafayette met early in 1800 to speak at length for the first time. Napoleon hoped that if they shared similar views on certain things, it would help

Jacques-Louis David painted this portrait of Napoleon, titled *Bonaparte Crossing the Alps at Grand-Saint-Bernard*, in 1800. He did four versions of the painting. Born in Corsica in 1769, Napoleon Bonaparte became emperor of France during the French Revolution. He was known for his skill as a military strategist, but he also took back much power from the French people and created a dictatorship.

his popularity. Unfortunately, they had very different opinions on everything. Despite being very hurt about not being invited to Washington's memorial service, Lafayette did not hate Napoleon. Napoleon and Lafayette even liked each other in a strange way. For many years, Napoleon and Lafayette maintained an odd relationship. They spoke often, but rarely would Napoleon acknowledge Lafayette's presence publicly. Lafayette had "dangerous" ideas, but privately Napoleon respected what he had done in America and his role in France since then. He offered Lafayette a seat in the Senate but Lafayette refused. In 1802, when France voted to make Napoleon first consul for life, Lafayette voted against him and told him so. Napoleon was still popular without Lafayette's support and was named emperor on December 2, 1804. As emperor of France, he continued his attempts to conquer the world.

Lafayette endured the worst time of his life in late 1807. On December 24, 1807, Adrienne, his beloved wife, died at the age of forty-eight. Lafayette was devastated. She had sacrificed her happiness for his many times over the course of her life. She deeply loved Lafayette, and Lafayette loved her deeply in return. At her burial, Lafayette told a friend, "Up to now, you have found me stronger than my circumstances; today, the circumstance is stronger than I." After her death, Lafayette blocked off her side of the house and nobody was permitted in the area for as long as he lived. Every morning he would spend fifteen minutes meditating while holding a portrait of her.

After Napoleon became emperor, people often asked Lafayette for comments about how Napoleon was ruling. Lafayette would rarely, if ever, criticize him. Napoleon was a great conqueror, even if he might not have been a great emperor. While leading France, Napoleon almost took over all of Europe until hitting a fierce Russian army and a fiercer Russian winter late in 1812. In the spring of 1812, Napoleon had entered Russia with six hundred thousand troops. Only ninety-three thousand returned.

This is the second of two paintings titled *Battle of Leipzig* by Friedrich Hoch, who lived between 1751 and 1812. This battle was a crushing defeat for Napoleon, especially following on the heels of the huge losses in Russia the winter before. Lafayette convinced the assembly that Napoleon needed to step down.

Allied armies again defeated Napoleon at the Battle of Leipzig, also known as the Battle of Nations, fought between October 16 and 19, 1813. This battle destroyed French power in Germany and Poland. More than thirty-eight thousand French were killed or wounded and thirty thousand more were captured. Lafayette demanded that Napoleon step down and convinced the public that France would be better off without Napoleon in power. The assembly also agreed. If Napoleon did not step down voluntarily he would be forcibly dethroned.

Napoleon left and went to Elba, where he arrived on May 4, 1814. He remained there for a short while, then returned to France in 1815. His return did drum up some enthusiasm and he attempted to take control again. He formed a small army but was defeated by Allied troops that severely outnumbered him. Parliament exiled him again, this time to the island of St. Helena, where he would remain until his death in 1821.

Louis XVIII took over the rule of France. Louis XVIII promised to be more liberal than leaders in the past, giving only limited power to the monarchy. Unfortunately, Louis XVIII's word was meaningless. Seeing this, Lafayette became more involved than ever before, trying to ensure that the French people had a voice in government. There were many small revolution attempts over the next few years and Lafayette's name was attached to most of them. Privately, Lafayette also

This oil painting of Louis XVIII is by Baron Francois Pascal Gerard, who lived from 1770 to 1837. The king, Louis-Stanislas-Xavier, was born in 1755 at Versailles. He used the deaths of Louis XVI and Marie Antoinette to promote himself as a successor to the throne should the Revolution be put down. After Napoleon's reign, the people of France were ready to receive him, especially because he promised to reform the government to give more power to the people.

donated money to small groups that chose to harass the people in power.

By 1824, the mood had turned conservative throughout France. Lafayette was even defeated in a general election that years earlier he would have won easily. He was still respected but realized that people were less likely to fight for the causes that had always been important to him. Lafayette was then sixty-six years old and looked forward to spending time running his farm and playing with his grandchildren.

9. His Final Years

Soon after Lafayette retired to his farm, U.S. president James Monroe invited him and his son, Georges, to come to America to celebrate its fiftieth year of independence. It would be his first visit in forty years. Lafayette could not refuse an offer to return to the country that he had grown to love so much.

Lafayette, along with his son, his secretary, and his valet, arrived in the United States on July 13, 1824. The United States was now comprised of twenty-four states and Lafayette visited each one. He symbolized the values on which America had been founded. Crowds went crazy wherever he went. Large numbers of people walked many miles (km) just for the privilege of seeing him. Lafayette gave many speeches and received gifts wherever he went. He also went to Washington's tomb in Mount Vernon to pay his respects to the man he had often viewed as the father he never had. During his visit, Congress also awarded

Opposite: This painting of Lafayette by Samuel F. B. Morse was painted between 1825 and 1828. It was probably started during Lafayette's visit to the United States between 1824 and 1825.

No. 3433

Office of Discount & Deposit of the Bank of the United States,

WASHINGTON, *Feby 16th* 1825

Cashier of the Bank of the United States,

Pay to the order of *General Lafayette*

One hundred twenty thousand dollars

$120.00 Q 100 Dollars.   *Tho. Swann, Prest.*

This is the original check that was given to Lafayette by the U.S. government as compensation for his services in the war for independence. It was endorsed and cashed through Nicholas Biddle Bank in Philadelphia on February 16, 1825.

Lafayette a large cash sum of about $120,000 or more and a grant of land in Florida.

Lafayette remained in the United States for more than a year. President John Quincy Adams was elected to office during Lafayette's stay. Near the end of Lafayette's trip, Adams persuaded Lafayette to stay through his sixty-ninth birthday. On the night before his birthday, Adams gave a farewell birthday party for Lafayette. When Lafayette left the next day, Adams said, "We shall look upon you always as belonging to us. During the whole of our life, and as belonging to our children after us . . . You are ours by that tie of love, stronger than death, which has linked your name for the endless ages of time with the name of Washington." Nothing Adams could have said would have meant more to Lafayette than being associated with George Washington, his friend and hero.

Lafayette returned to France on October 3, 1825. Louis XVIII had died and Charles X was now king of France. Charles X was hostile and distrustful of Lafayette. Charles X was also very unpopular because he wanted to restore absolute power to the monarchy. Charles X took away voting privileges from all people except the wealthy. Lafayette got very upset when Charles X disbanded the National Guard. Because of all the major problems he saw in government, Lafayette wanted more power to change things. When a spot opened in Parliament, Lafayette took it. In response, Charles X disbanded Parliament, as well as any newspapers that supported liberty. Another revolution was brewing.

In July 1830, France began another short revolution and Lafayette, at age seventy-three, was in the middle of it. The primary reason for the revolution was the passing of the July Ordinances. These ordinances controlled the press, dissolved the newly elected Chamber of Deputies, and reduced the people's voting power. The revolution soon ended, as did the reign of Charles X, who abdicated the throne and fled the country. On July 31, the Duke of Orleans, Louis-Philippe, took the throne with the promise of creating

This undated engraving shows Charles X, who lived from 1757 to 1836. Charles X became king after the death of Louis XVIII in 1824. He favored Roman Catholicism and the aristocracy during his reign. This caused great opposition and led to a rebellion in 1830, forcing Charles X to resign and flee to Britain.

a republic. Lafayette endorsed him. He was hopeful that Louis-Philippe would govern under the principles Lafayette had written about fifty years earlier in the "Declaration of the Rights of Man and Citizen." Louis-Philippe took control with the support of Lafayette and the people.

While Louis-Philippe was in power, Lafayette returned to his rank as commander of the National Guard. Lafayette had participated in his third revolution and had commanded the Army of National Guards that drove Charles X from France. Upon taking power, Louis-Philippe became very insecure and began turning to the aristocrats for support. He was jealous of Lafayette's popularity and was doing many things with which Lafayette did not agree. Lafayette resigned his post in the National Guard on December 25, 1830.

Lafayette then spent most of his time making speeches of protest whenever the government did something that he did not like. When not speaking in Parliament, Lafayette spent a lot of time on his estate with his family and writing his memoirs. Writing a history of his life proved to be a very large project. He had written almost three thousand pages by the time he was finished.

In February 1834, Lafayette became ill after attending a funeral service for a friend. It was cold and damp, and he was seventy-six, but Lafayette insisted on walking behind the procession without a

Louis-Philippe was the Duke of Orleans before he became king of France after Charles X was forced to abdicate. Louis-Philippe reigned from 1830 to 1848. Although the king was a constitutional monarch, he gained considerable personal power by splitting the liberal movement and appointing weak ministers, such as Louis Molé.

hat. Lafayette got very sick as a result of a simple gesture designed to show respect for his friend. His illness quickly worsened into pneumonia. Lafayette recovered later in the spring but after going out once more he got caught in a thunderstorm and got sick again. That time, he did not recover. Lafayette died on May 20, 1834, holding a miniature locket that held a picture of Adrienne. He was surrounded by the members of his family, including his dog.

Lafayette was buried in Picpus Cemetery next to Adrienne. American soil, which he had brought back from America in 1825, was tossed on his coffin.

This is a color lithograph by A. Maugendre titled *Sépulture du Général Lafayette et de sa Famille*. It shows Lafayette's tomb in Picpus Cemetery, Paris, where he was buried next to Adrienne.

America declared official mourning throughout the country upon learning of Lafayette's death. President Andrew Jackson ordered the same military honors that Washington had received. Salutes were fired at every army post in the nation and on every ship. Flags were lowered to half-mast and memorial services were held throughout America. Lafayette, hero of France and of the United States, had died.

10. Lafayette's Legacy

Lafayette was a hero at a time when there were few heroes. Most leaders were corrupt, but the people were powerless to do anything. Lafayette spent his entire life trying to give power to those people who had none. He did it through his actions, by fighting for the colonists in the American Revolution, and he did it through his words, by speaking against the government in France for fifty years. Despite all the troubles in France over the course of his life, Lafayette was always optimistic and believed liberty would triumph over all. On January 2, 1834, in his last major speech, Lafayette said, "Republicanism is the sovereignty of the people . . . There are natural and imprescriptible rights that an entire nation has no right to violate."

People were always drawn to Lafayette's words and actions. This is illustrated by the participation of Francis Huger in Lafayette's attempted escape from Olmutz prison. While leaving the home of Major Huger on his first visit to the U.S., Lafayette bent down and patted Huger's five-year-old son on the cheek. It was an innocent gesture, but the child never forgot his warmth and genuine kindness. When the opportunity arose twenty years later for him to help Lafayette, he jumped at the opportunity. Lafayette needed help after being jailed and the boy, now a man, was willing to risk his life to aid in the escape of this great hero.

Lafayette's children never had his charisma or chose to live a public life. His son, Georges, was always comfortable living in his father's great shadow until after his father's death. When Lafayette died, so great was Georges's respect for his father that he collected all of his father's records, speeches, and letters. He spent the rest of his life protesting any misrepresentation of his father and his ideals. Though more comfortable living a private life, he felt obligated to make sure that his father's legacy was known to those who did not experience it while Lafayette lived.

Lafayette symbolized virtue for the American people and received a great deal of glory because of it. Americans always felt virtue would be needed in a successful republican government and they felt that Lafayette, a foreigner who believed in their cause, was the best example that they had of virtue. Lafayette's actions throughout his life never made the Americans regret their decision to glorify him. He was someone who always was true to the cause of the common people, displaying virtue each and every day of his life.

This portrait shows Georges Washington Lafayette, the son of Marquis de Lafayette. Georges, like his father, experienced life in two worlds. He was of French birth and spent much of his life there, but he was sent to America during his family's imprisonment in Austria. He also toured America with his father from 1824 to 1825. Georges did not have the same ambition for glory as did his father, but he worked very hard after his father's death to preserve Lafayette's memory.

Lafayette's memory lives on in America through the many towns, buildings, streets, and universities that share his name. This photograph is one example. This is the Lafayette Hilton in Lafayette, Louisiana.

Lafayette was a defender of freedom at the expense of everything else. He was fearless and principled, and he embodied freedom. Many streets, hotels, and schools in the United States and in France continue to bear his name. Lafayette, a hero to two nations, remains buried in France where the U.S. flag has flown over his grave since his death.

Timeline

1757	On September 6, Marie Joseph Paul Yves Roch Gilbert du Motier de Lafayette is born.
1774	In April, Lafayette marries Adrienne.
1775	On April 19, the American Revolution begins at Lexington and Concord.
	In December, Henriette is born.
1777	In April, Lafayette sails for America to help the colonists fight against Britain.
	In July, Anastasie is born.
	Lafayette arrives in Philadelphia to join the Continental army.
	In September, Lafayette joins the troops
	Lafayette fights in his first battle, the Battle of Brandywine.

In November, Lafayette leads a raid against Hessian troops in New Jersey.

In December, Lafayette is given his own regiment to command.

1778	In June, Lafayette participates in the Battle of Monmouth.
1779	In February, Lafayette returns to France.

In December, Georges Washington de Lafayette is born.

1780	In April, Lafayette returns to America.
1781	In October, Lafayette participates in the Battle of Yorktown.
1782	In January, Lafayette returns to France.

In September, Virginie is born.

1783	The Treaty of Paris ends the Revolutionary War.
1789	In July, French citizens storm the Bastille prison.

Lafayette is named commander of the National Guard.

1791 In September, Louis XVI makes France a constitutional monarchy.

1792 In August, Lafayette is jailed after Jacobins overthrow French government.

1794 In November, Lafayette attempts and fails to escape from prison.

1795 In October, Adrienne, Anastasie, and Virginie join Lafayette in prison.

1797 In September, Lafayette and his family are released from prison.

1799 In October, Lafayette returns to France.

1804 In December, Napoleon is named emperor of France.

1807 In December, Adrienne dies.

1824 In July, Lafayette and his son, Georges, visit the United States.

1825 In October, Lafayette returns home.

1830 In July, revolution breaks out in France.

Lafayette again becomes commander of the National Guard in France but resigns in the same year.

1834 In May, Lafayette dies.

Glossary

abdicate (AB-dih-kayt) To formally surrender a throne.

absurd (ub-SERD) Something so unreasonable that it would appear ridiculous.

affiliate (uh-FIH-lee-ayt) To associate oneself with a group.

alliance (uh-LY-uhnts) A close association formed between people or groups of people to reach a common objective.

ambassador (am-BA-suh-der) The highest-ranking representative of one country assigned to conduct relations with another country.

amputate (AM-pyoo-tayt) To cut off or remove, especially the removal of a limb by surgery.

aristocrat (uh-RIS-tuh-krat) A member of the upper class or nobility.

barricaded (BA-ruh-kayd-ed) Fortified with an obstacle that hinders the approach of an enemy.

betrayer (bih-TRAY-er) One who delivers something into the hands of an enemy by violating trust.

cockade (kaw-KAYD) A knot of ribbon, or something similar, worn on the hat as a badge.

commission (kuh-MIH-shun) An official certificate giving military rank or authority.

defiance (di-FY-uhnts) Open resistance to authority.

desertion (di-ZER-shun) Giving up one's position or cause; abandonment.

disband (dis-BAND) To break up an organization.

disperse (dih-SPURS) To scatter in all directions.

encampment (en-KAMP-ment) The place where a group of troops has set up a camp or campsite.

feudal privileges (FYOO-dul PRIV-lij-ez) Voting rights based on land ownership.

fortify (FOR-tih-fy) To strengthen and secure something, or to provide something with works of defense.

harassment (huh-RAS-mint) The act of tormenting someone.

hereditary (huh-REH-dih-teh-ree) A trait that is passed down by an ancestor from generation to generation.

Hessian (HEH-shen) A German professional soldier who served in the British army for pay in the Revolutionary War.

imprescriptible (im-pruh-SKRIP-tuh-bul) Something that is not able to be lost or taken away.

inhabit (in-HA-bit) To occupy as a place of residence.

inhabitants (in-HA-buh-tents) People who stay in a specific place or region.

maturity (muh-TYUR-uh-tee) A state of full development, either mentally or physically.

memoirs (MEM-wars) An account of happenings, usually biographical, based on personal observation.

mercenary (MER-suhn-er-ee) Any professional soldier serving in a foreign army for pay.

moderate (MOH-duh-ret) A person whose views or opinions are within reasonable bounds; avoiding excesses or extremes.

morale (moh-RAL) Having confidence and enthusiasm.

musket (MUS-kit) A long-barreled firearm used by soldiers before the invention of the rifle.

mutiny (MYOO-tin-ee) A revolt of a crew, or of soldiers against their commanding officer or officers.

obligation (ah-bluh-GAY-shun) A duty imposed legally or socially; something one has to do.

offensive (uh-FENT-siv) Attacking another.

oppressed (uh-PRESD) Being kept down by cruel or unjust use of power or authority.

ordinance (OR-duh-nunts) A law set forth by a person or an authority.

protégé (PRO-tuh-zhay) One who is trained, supported, or sponsored by another.

province (PRAH-vunts) A region, district, or territory.

radical (RA-dih-kuhl) A person in politics who favors extreme change.

reconcile (REH-kun-syl) To settle a quarrel or fight.

redoubt (rih-DOWT) A temporary fortification used to secure hilltops, passes, or the flanks of entrenchments.

regiment (REH-juh-muhnt) A military unit.

reinforcements (ree-in-FORS-muhnts) Anything that strengthens, specifically additional troops or warships to make stronger those already sent.

representation (reh-prih-zen-TAY-shun) When people are elected to the government to do what the voters want them to do.

resolution (reh-zuh-LOO-shun) A formal statement adopted by a group of people.

scurvy (SKER-vee) A disease resulting from a deficiency of vitamin C, characterized by weakness and bleeding from mucous membranes.

skirmish (SKER-mish) A brief fight or encounter.

stipend (STY-pehnd) A small periodic payment or compensation.

unanimously (yoo-NA-nih-mus-lee) Agreeing completely; having all parties in agreement.

unconditional (un-kun-DISH-ih-nul) Without conditions or reservations; absolute.

valet (va-LAY) A personal servant.

violate (VY-uh-layt) To break a law or a rule.

Additional Resources

If you would like to learn more about Marquis de Lafayette, check out the following books and Web sites:

Books

Brandt, Keith. *Lafayette: Hero of Two Nations.* New York: Trell Associates, 1990.

Fritz, Jean. *Why Not, Lafayette?* New York: G.P. Putnam's Sons, a Division of Penguin Putnam, 1999.

Grote, Joann. *Lafayette: French Freedom Fighter*. New York: Chelsea House Publishing, 2000.

Web Sites

www.chateau-lafayette.com/us/indexus.htm

ww2.lafayette.edu/~library/special/exhibits/olmutz/olmutz.html

www.ushistory.org/valleyforge/served/lafayette.html

Bibliography

Bernier, Olivier. *Lafayette, Hero of Two Worlds*. New York: E.P. Dutton, Inc., 1983.

Carlton, Bronwyn. *The Big Book of Death*. Brooklyn, NY: Paradox Press, 1995.

Gottschalk, Louis, and Maddox, Margaret. *Lafayette in the French Revolution*. Chicago: The University of Chicago Press, 1973.

Gottschalk, Louis. *Lafayette Joins the American Army*. Chicago: The University of Chicago Press, 1965.

Karapaides, Harry J. *Dates of the American Revolution*. Shippensburg: Burd Street Press, 1998.

Latzko, Andreas. *Lafayette, A Life*. New York: Country Life Press, 1936.

Loveland, Anne C. *Lafayette, Emblem of Liberty*. Baton Rouge: Louisiana State University Press, 1971.

Sedgwick, Henry Dwight. *Lafayette*. Brooklyn, NY: The Bobbs-Merrill Company, 1928.

Woodward, W. E. *Lafayette*. New York: Farrar & Rinehart, Inc., 1938.

Index

About the Author

Greg Payan, who received his Bachelor of Arts in journalism, is a freelance writer who lives in New York with his wife, Casey. He was interested in writing about Lafayette in order to better understand the relationship between France and America during the Revolution. Greg's father was born and raised in France, so Lafayette's heritage was particularly interesting to Greg. He wanted more in-depth knowledge of what Lafayette meant to America and France.

Credits

Series Design

Laura Murawski

Layout Design

Corinne Jacob

Project Editor

Joanne Randolph